AF572653

GRANDPARENTS ARE SPECIAL

GRANDPARENTS ARE SPECIAL

Jessie Merle Franklin

BROADMAN PRESS/NASHVILLE, TENNESSEE

4256-39
ISBN: 0-8054-5639-2

Dewey Decimal Classification: 811
Subject heading: GRANDPARENTS—POETRY

Library of Congress Catalog Card Number: 79-51761
Printed in the United States of America

Contents

FOREWORD

Soon after the initial giddiness of becoming one, I began to think seriously about grandparents. Who are they and what are they for? What are the individuals who comprise this group like? How are they similar to and different from other persons? And what is the purpose of their God-given role? I say "God-given" because I am a firm believer with the Preacher of Ecclesiastes 3:1: "To everything there is a season, and a time to every purpose under the heaven."

Then as writers are prone to do, I began to write. Some of the ideas expressed here sprang full grown from my heart, like Minerva from the head of Zeus. Some were lifted tenderly from the treasure trove of memory. Still others were born of observation. In some instances, it was necessary for me to "walk a mile in another's moccasins" in order to speak from that one's point of view. Each experience has added to the interest and worth, I trust, of the lines offered here.

I never intended nor expected this to be a profound treatise on human behavior. But I have hoped from the beginning that every grandparent who reads it will feel a warm glow of identity with its gentle words and feelings, and will thereby be able to relive the sheer delight that grandparenthood is.

Jessie Merle Franklin

Who are grandparents?

They are people . . .

. . . Tall and short. (Over this they have no control, unless, of course, they notice they seem to be getting shorter of late. Maybe that needs looking into.)

. . . Thin and fat. (Mostly the latter, with strange new settlings and bulges, which they work at dutifully, leaving cream and sugar out of their coffee and taking such brisk walks that they must have a little extra snack afterward to sustain them.)

. . .Just ordinary people. Well—almost.

Grandparents Are the Ones—

You can run to, laugh and weep with,
Have neat secrets you can keep with,
Hoe the garden, cook or sweep with,
And be quiet beside to sleep with;
You can show a trick or treasure
And they'll oh and ah with pleasure;
They can help you plan and measure,
Or if you want to, you just *leisure.*

Grandparents Have to Write It Down

My grandmother can't remember where
She laid her purse or glasses down,
Or if she left her keys at home
Or where she parked the car downtown.
But she can remember lots about
When she was a girl and still in swing
In prehistoric days before
TV and space or anything.

My granddad asks us something over
We told him just the other day;
He says because most people mumble
So you can't hear what they say.
But he can remember important subjects
Like how he rode an old gray mule
Delivering papers in the dawn
Then loping all the way to school.

Grandparents have to write down dates
And telephone numbers and where to go;
And when they are asked about such stuff,
They have to check or they won't know.
But I don't care if they forget
The things that others keep in mind.
I'm glad it's neat, remembered things
They don't have trouble trying to find.

Once *they* were the grandchildren (and it's a treasured memory, let me tell you, that brings an ache to the heart and a lump to the throat).

I Remember—

The heady excitement of dressing up and walking the mile and a half into town and back with my grandmother just to eat at the cafe—"a dozen fried" for her and a hamburger for me.

The sheer contentment of sitting on her front porch shaded from the afternoon sun while spooning from a platter watering mouthfuls of her beaten, still-warm candy to which there was no taste comparable this side of heaven.

The peace of going to sleep on hot summer nights, cleaned of a child's play grime and lying beside her in her bed that smelled of sun and air, lulled to drowsiness by the steady stream of cool wind from the wielded fan in her hand.

Tiptoeing to peek into her dining room safe, luxuriating in its pineapple-cake, baked-biscuit smell that mingled with the aroma of honeysuckle on the wooden trellis outside the wide west window panes on which stray bits of sun were shimmering through the green.

Listening to her colloquialisms like "mommick" and "ready as calf," and liking them; liking, too her earthy humor and enthralling stories about her girlhood trek to Texas in a wagon and the Civil War days when a stranger left a bag of gold in her father's keep, which went unopened until the owner returned.

Seated on a willow pond bank with her through a lazy summer afternoon to fish with string for crawfish, and later relishing the sweet-tasting tails she had rolled in cornmeal and fried.

Playing hull-gull or hide-the-thimble with her while rain gurgled from the gutters outside, filling the big round kitchen cistern; or north winds whined like dogs to get in by her warm fireplace.

n't it just yesterday?) the grandparents now were the rents rearing a family.

God's Blessed Thought

As long as dads do what dads do
And still can grin and call out, "Boo!"
And swing a squealing youngster high
Until he touches stardust sky—
Can share with sons his favorite haunts
And build a cabinet Mom wants—
Can mend a kite and buy a pup
And turn the whole world right side up—

As long as moms do what moms do—
Clean up the house and make a stew
And carry gigglers here and there
And still somehow find time to spare
To zip a zipper—blow a nose
And put a bandaid on life's woes—
Can make each day a sandwich spread
With love between two laughs of bread—

As long as kids do what kids do
With guardian angels seeing them through—
Can spat among themselves and weep
Then look like cherubs in their sleep,
And troubled from without can stick
With loyalty that is fierce and quick—
Can grow up finally and roam
Yet still find joy in "going home"—

As long as there are these, there will be
God's blessed thought—a family.

And just yesterday the grandparents of today were the ones being diplomatically patient with their grandparent (or vice versa!).

Heart Reels

We place her rocking chair up center front
To hold her china thinness, help her hunt
Her spectacles, then when she signals ready,
Snap off the lights and start. "That one is Teddy,
Grandmother," someone yells (her hearing is bad),
Or, "See, Grandmother, that's the baby with Dad."
"Yes, I can see," she says, "they're mighty fine.
They didn't have home movies, though, when mine
Were small, so I just have to try to remember—
I recollect one day—it was in December—"
"Grandmother," we shout, "the pictures aren't through yet."
"Oh, yes," she says, "excuse me. I forget."
And so she patiently waits till ours are shown
So she can run off heart reels of her own.

Grandparents ache a lot with arthritis in their extremities and world conditions in their hearts. Sometimes they cry over things like remembering, or newspaper stories about little children. Or being too happy, and saying hellos and goodbyes. But they laugh a lot, too (mostly chuckles), sometimes at themselves.

Birds of a Feather

"The years fly by," the sages sigh,
"It's something you just have to weather."
But the flock I know never did go;
They stayed and now roost together.

Uncle Sam

He was often my father's visitor,
A tall, white-whiskered man of noble mien.
I still can see my father giving him respectful attention.
I would gravely shake his hand
And always sit as close to his chair as I could,
Listening in awe to his kindly, beaming voice.
My father called him "Uncle Sam,"
And though nobody ever told me his full name,
I felt sure I knew.
And so I gave him his merited place of honor in my heart.

When I came to realize
He was just a family friend—
Not national in scope at all—
It was too late.
He was and is and will always be to me
In memory
"Uncle Sam, United States of America"
Salute!

Favorite Chair

To look at it was restful; it had sat
So many through the years. It sagged a bit,
Just enough for comfort and for fit,
And had a leeward lean as though to chat.

It held the winter sun like a heating pad,
And rocked in shady breeze when summer came.
"We must get rid of it!" we would exclaim,
But somehow through the years we never had.

And then today I said again, "This minute
I'll scheme a scheme and get it out of sight!"
But even as I planned its banished plight,
Guess who was in deep comfort sitting in it.

And sometimes grandparents chuckle over things with others.

Roosting

We can't see why these few old chickens make
A fuss about having to go to bed
In the henhouse every night. You'd think instead
Of grumbling, they'd be glad, but they still shake
The tree limbs, flapping up there one by one,
Pushing and teetering and falling until the sun
Has tucked its head beneath a wing. Then when
We have shooed and got them down and try to steer
Them like sleepwalkers to their roost, they peer
With longing necks back toward the tree. One hen,
A stubborn, transgressing Lot's wife to the end,
Dashes back, refusing to be penned.
We hear her in the treetop, fume and mince
At settling until the summer moon, as round
As an orange rises; then she drops toward ground,
And does a tightrope walk along the fence.
And though she is unrepentant of her sin,
We go out and let her, squawking, in.

Given the chance, grandparents have been known to travel quite a bit (carefully in their own cars and campers; on buses, where they sleep peacefully through miles of scenery; and on planes, where they pray a lot). Why do they travel so much? Maybe it is partly because of the gypsy that is in all of us.

Dog in a Pickup

He stood with front paws resting on a rise,
nose pointing into the wind
and long hair rippling
like a Viking in the prow of his boat
as it sailed out to some unknown far off land.

And seeing him, I felt a sudden yen
to leave convention behind,
and with hair loosened
and streaming, and face into the wind,
to travel, too, to some adventure waiting.

Maybe, again, grandparents travel to dots on yellowed maps that were carefully folded and put away during the demanding years of parenthood—to "faraway places with strange sounding names" they have always silently yearned to see. So now they can. And do.

And they marvel at and snap pictures of the things they see, yearning all the while to have all their relatives and friends there with them.

Land of Aloha

Not far away by a great jet's wing
Is a paradise land of eternal spring,
A land of rhythmic sounds and songs
Like the waves of the sea to which it belongs—
The land of the fragrant lei.

King Kamehameha, eight feet tall,
Lives on in the proud-borne surfers, all
Like sun-bronzed gods. The snorklers dive
Where the brilliantly colored fishes thrive—
In Hanauma Bay.

In the land of Aloha and the monkeypod tree,
Breathtaking colors in flowers and sea—
Where Haleakala once glowed red,
And Pearl Harbor holds its gallant war dead—
We saw Jesus, too.

In a little church where we went to pray
When Sunday came, He had come to stay
In the hearts of a people with golden skin—
And we worshiped with them and felt akin,
For theirs was the Christ we knew.

The Fishermen of Cascais

The fishermen of Cascais have made
a catch. Boa pescaria! The news
flows in ahead of them and sweeps across
the ancient fishing village mouth to mouth—
from laughter to laughter—from shout to shout—then ebbs
back like the tide to meet the fishermen as
they row their crude, rough boats to shore.
All night
they have fought until the Old Man of the Sea
grew tired, and once again the fishermen
of Cascais have won. Prince Henry, ahoy!
And Vasca de Gama, log this day! Your sons
have won, and now they trot in pairs on bare
red feet as crusty as barnacles, faces grey
with salt above their coarse knit sweaters. What
burden does each stretcher bear that bows
their sturdy backs? Sardines! A basket, black
and bulging! Into the waiting donkey cart
dump your precious load, and away in a trot
again to the boats for another. Ho! No one
can doubt it now. Today's catch is indeed
a good one. Shout it back and forth, and kiss
one cheek, then the other! No idle fisherman's tale
is this today!

Now come the thick-limbed wives.
Like shrieking gulls they gather about the fish,
each vying for another meal to take
away in her net bag. So let them laugh!
And hug, and chatter. How often have they stood,
bone-chilled and silent in the cold grey dawn,
to wait for ships that never did return,
or returning, told their tale of broken nets
or nets left empty by a sullen Old
Man of the Sea.
The carts grow full and soon
the donkeys clop away. The fishermen see
to their nets, and as excitement lulls at last,
amid the maze of boats and hanging ropes,
a hoary fisherman sits and nods, his crust
of hard bread in his lap, his jug of wine
slung over one shoulder. Has not the Sculptor told
his story in stone above all Lisbon? How
the Old Man of the Sea so huge and fierce
is ever there to devour him? Nap while you can,
Old One. Tomorrow is another time,
but today a thousand diamonds glitter out
in the peaceful bay.
A lone fish wife is left,
her stocky body a weathered boat with great
thick mast. She has hailed and kissed and jabbered more
than any. Now she leaves to push her hand cart
through the cobbled streets. She hawks her wares
in sweet triumph like a prayer that wails and wafts
above the red tile roofs. "Good ca-atch! Good ca-atch!"

As they travel, grandparents make friends wherever they go. And if they weren't sure before, they become thoroughly convinced that people are the same, no matter where you find them.

In a Church in Nassau

Black she was with dignity and grace
From some ancestral Sheba. Each in place,
Her children sat beside her in a row,
Their ebon skin against white clothes aglow.
And in the stone church, windows opened wide,
The blackness rose and spread, a rolling tide
That washed us, two white pebbles, ashore with scorn
For those who were made white when they were born.
My heart stood still. Is this the way *they* feel
When white acts as if only white is real?
The litany began and soon my plight
Of being without a Bible caught her sight,
And turning with a quiet, gentle air,
She lent me hers as if to say, "I care."

Elijah Was His Name

We met a man in Bethlehem
Of swarthy skin and flashing smile;
Elijah was his name.
And as he talked
We could hear the hooves of Arabian stallions
  thundering through the rock-strewn hills—
His Ishmael's fierce and burning pride.

But more
We felt a spirit touched by Christ.
It was as though he threw his cape around our shoulders,
Killed a choice sheep for our stay,
Then laid his chief's sword by our beds
As dark lay early on Judean hills.
But most of all
We felt his passionate love for truth,
Verse by Bible verse, leading the way
Along the ancient simple paths where Jesus walked—
Breaking shackles of half truths—
Until our listening hearts lay hushed and still,
And thrilled within us with
A surer faith.

Mainly, of course, grandparents disturb their sleep and bathroom habits, and start to worry about things at home even before they get to where they are going, because their children and grandchildren are "way over there." So they sit a little tense and apprehensive over incredible miles of land and water to get to see them.

Grandparents are lovable (that is, most of them are). There aren't any human angels walking around here on earth, you know, not even gray-haired ones with dentures. But through some eyes, grandparents come close.

In Granddad's Yard

Today I played in Granddad's yard and saw a lot of things
That ran and crawled and jumped around, and flew on magic wings.
A big black bug with helmet on rode on his Honda fast
Right down the driveway, while above, with amplifiers full blast,
A bird rock group sang in the trees. And next, an athlete flea
Broke all world flea jump records with a leap from Shep to me.
Some doodle bugs in little houses in the shady dirt
Came out when I called down to them, "Your children will get hurt!"
A dragon fly ski-ed back and forth across the birdbath lake,
And two ant teams played scrimmage when I dropped a crumb of cake.
A spider paratrooper fell and dangled where he hung
Upon a bush, and in the shiny sunbeam where he swung,
Some silly girl gnats danced ballet; then straight into the sun
A grasshopper launched his rocket as I counted down to one.
And when I told her, my grandmother said, "Well, mercy me!"
And my granddad said, "Who'd a-thought all that was there to see!"

To grandparents, love is indeed "a many splendored thing." It has been theirs to cherish since the tenderness of spring.

Old House in the Rain

A prankish wind has fingered up a shingle,
And a raindrop cane is tapping in the attic.
The odor of cool, washed air drifts in to mingle
With the smell of burning logs. Are we erratic
To sit here unperturbed before the fire?
Some might think so. We'll have to climb tomorrow
To mend where age and elements conspire,
But here tonight there is no age nor sorrow,
Just you and I and love—the dripping shutters—
The soothing, rain-wet chuckle of the gutters.

Love has walked beside most grandparents in the busy days of summer, and it has raced with them through the gold and orange flame of autumn.

Autumn Paths

Come race with me down an autumn path
as once again we are young
With faces lifted in the rain
and laughter thrown to wind—
Race on until the mellow sun,
like golden honey thinned,
Spills out across the leaves that lie
like gypsy beads unstrung.
Ah, autumn is the time when spring's
green promise can be claimed,
And we will find it, you and I,
up hillsides copper flamed.

And with some, love still abides in the quieter strength of the days of their winter.

Love Letter Written in Snow

"You stay in bed awhile," he calls aloud,
And I am glad to this one morning. Snow
Is caped around the shoulders of the yard
And fastened with one round gate button. A shroud
Of mystery cloaks the familiar winding row
Of fence posts beyond where still unmarred
The fields sleep under blankets. A neighboring barn
Pokes out an inquiring roof, and elf and sprite
That stand where tree and bush once grew are dressed
In dazzling knitted suits of snowflake yarn.
The fire he built leaps up in warm delight
And drowsily I think how I am blessed.

In addition to their own ever-widening family circle, grandparents have divided love with many others through the years. There are the friends that have grown grey along with them.

Will It Suffice?

How can we find right words, enough to tell
You of the love that is in our hearts, dear friends?
For sometimes words are inadequate and dispel
Emotion's richness even though one bends
Them carefully on love's potter's wheel and spends
Long hours drying in kiln of the soul.
If we could only find where a rainbow ends,
Or know divine truth here revealed in whole,
If we could fathom faith's eternal goal,
Or see the wonder in a small child's heart,
Or share an actor's most magnificent role—
Then we might tell our love for you in part.
  Will it suffice perhaps if we just say
  We hold you in a warm and caring way?

There were those who grew special to them as they exchanged back-door visits.

To Neighbors Moved Away

The moving van has gone, and we stand here,
This suddenly quiet, deserted house and I.
They have not moved away is what it is saying,
See that stack of magazines there by
The door? So pretending, it keeps warm
Your presence in each lonesome, empty room,
Where silence creaks and whispers in alarm.
Something as fragile as sharing fireside dreams,
And yet as real as digging in damp garden
Earth together, ended when you left
Today. No more to hear your cheerful song
In the kitchen! No more to borrow this and that,
And lingering, bring back warmth and love along
With flour! The roses that we shared, your cat
That slept in our garage—all of these
Are over, and you are really gone, I know,
But in this moment here, *it cannot be so!*

There were the household help, who returned love and loyalty in such measure, the check that passed between them monthly seemed but a secondary gesture.

Bertha

Bertha is jolly and full of bounce
Concocting cobbler with "buttered juice"
Or giving ironed things "front row flounce,"
But she lets righteous anger loose
In elbow zeal and thunderous face
When rounding up the dirt which she
Says "seems like immigrates" a place.
Sometimes Bertha "leaves us be"
A week or more, then she is back
To "heist" things up where they belong,
Measure heartstrings, "take up slack,"
And soothe the house with hums of song.

And there are the many who now await them on the "other side."

Erma

Erma stepped softly,
but she is missed like all the gentle things of life
when they are gone—
  a ripple of breeze
  a hum of song
  a murmur of love—
all of these touch the heart with beauty's brush
and leave a poignant tint
that never fades.
Erma stepped softly,
and the echoes of her footsteps do not thunder
down the corridors of time,
but they tiptoe
  with all life's quieter things
  in the gentle places of our hearts.

Perhaps better than anyone else, grandparents understand how "love divided multiplies."

To a Little Girl With Her Jealous Bone Exposed

Come, child, and let us try to allay your fears.
We would not scold you, for in your young mind
The special ones whose love you claim, it appears
Are being traitors, giving love in kind,
So it must seem to you, to a little boy
They scarcely know. Come, let us hold you tight,
So you can feel our love till small-girl joy
Returns, and once again your world glows bright.
Oh, we would teach you love does not grow smaller
When it is shared, but only deeper and taller.

As to their own needs, grandparents are proud and independent (and as transparent as cellophane).

What Do You Give Somebody Who Has Everything?

They don't need robes and they don't need ties—
Nor house shoes in a comfortable size,
Not shaving lotions or perfumes
Nor more accessories for their rooms.
Though grandparents always act delighted
Over each new present sighted,
Later in its jar or box
They store each one in a chest that locks
Or set it back high on a shelf
With a dozen others like itself.
Then when their children fume and fret
Because they don't use what they get,
They say, "We will," then drop their eyes
Where all the time the answer lies.
If only their loved ones would heed
It's plain as day what grandparents need.

Grandparents are still dreamers, but not in the sense of the fragile, illusive dreams of childhood and youth.

Creek Bed Sand

There was a place as a child I sat
Where a stream had traveled swiftly at that,
Till the sand it left was sugar white
And creamed to a velvet smooth delight.
And as I dug in, hands and toes,
And held it to trickle past my nose,
I only knew then it was good
To have a seat out in the wood,
To share the cleanness of the sand
And to mold its coolness in my hand.

Ah, sobering thoughts come soon enough
To aging hearts with aches and stuff,
And oh, how sweet to sit as a child
With trees umbrellaed and breezes mild!
Nobody told me, or needed to,
That God created all things true.
Nor did I think some day to pen
A poem about it, though I felt then
The wonder of Him who sculptured sand
As soft as a dream in a child's cupped hand.

Grandparents' dreams are as solid and real as life itself and as bright as the substance of faith.

Grandparents' Dreams

Grandparents' dreams are not great ships
that sail
to far off ports
or wild birds in their flight,
not untamed horses thundering down a trail
or ephemeral fireflies
flickering
in the night.
Their dreams are anchored solidly
in earth;
they are gentled horses
munching in their stalls
or birds in nests they build to shelter birth
and sing their songs of praise
whatever
befalls.
Mostly grandparents' dreams are like
the glow
of light from a city
set upon a hill
so other travelers near and dear may know
how high their dreams for them
how bright
how still.

Grandparents also have mountains yet to climb. To some of them it may mean something as grand as a Grandma Moses painting her incomparable primitives. To others it may be something as beautifully simple as crocheting a colorful afghan to give away. Or planting a garden to share with friends and neighbors.

Fall Garden

The old bent farmer was kin to the earth
With eyes of steady, honest blue.
"You enjoy gardening, don't you?" I asked,
And he answered, "Yessum, I reckon I do."

"I can understand why," I said with a wave
At the vegetables stretching row by row.
"It must be gratifying to watch
The things that you have planted grow."

"It's worth the worry," he said with a smile,
"Which in the spring is middlin' fair.
You plant and loosen the soil a mite,
And the rain and the sunshine make it bear.

"But in the fall—well now, there's more—
It takes some hustle and bustle and do,
For a body's some likely to want to sit
When the summer heat and sweat is through.

"But a fall garden's fresher and greener, seems like,
And the vegetables seem sweeter to taste,
Like maybe the good Lord's telling us all
It ain't a season you'd want to waste."

Whether it be a seemingly impenetrable Ararat with its ghostly hulk of an ark nestled in centuries of mystery and snow, or only a gently sloping hill with a meandering trail, grandparents know life's mountains never end. They stand squarely in every path, each with its challenge. Each with its element of risk and danger. And each with its bright reward.

What Is Your Mountain?

What is your mountain?
Climb it, friend.
But why?
To hear the wings
Of singing things.
To hold a parasol of sky
To see the awesome size of things
Up high.
And if it is one God chose for you.
You will never have a grander view.

"The children expect us," is the way grandparents explain away many things. Or "the grandchildren need us." So they sneak an extra nap (in bed it's called "lying down a spell" and in a chair, "resting my eyes"). Then they put on the most comfortable clothes they can find and are ready to be off to whatever comes—picnic, zoo, birthday party, Christmas play, piano recital, baseball game, and on and on. They go along grunting and blowing and complaining at times of being old or getting old. And loving dearly every huffing, puffing minute of it!

What Are Grandparents For?

Now that we have briefly explored who grandparents are, let's consider what they are *for*—their purpose for being. There are many roles in life to which they have been called to give time, talents and spiritual gifts through the years, and are still being called. But we might as well face it without further ado. Grandparents are, in the main, for grandchildren. They know it. And grandchildren know it. Each is pluperfectly, splendiforously, outrageously "grand" to the other. And there is nothing on earth quite like it!

Where Love Is

I remember a child now gray
Who ate two lunches every day,
At home and then the one she ate
By slipping through a picket gate,
And gazing with a longing eye
At tall-built cake or thick plump pie,
Then chatting over her own slice
Like little Sugar-Spice-and-Nice.

Although her grandmother was aware
Of the small deceit that brought her there,
She seemed to revel in her stay
And hugged her boarder every day
Till others, learning of the trend,
With grown-up logic, brought its end.
Where they think love is, others go,
But all grandchildren seem to know.

Coming Over

When I see him galloping there,
The little pony with reddish hair,
And the old man driving him over the plain,
(Strange horse, giggling!) and then again,
I leave a task half done to curl
With book and doll and a little girl,
I understand it when they say,
"Grandmother, we're coming over to play."

In the very beginning, grandparents are for adding their own special brand of welcome to the tiny squirming bundle that is their grandchild. It starts in the glow of expectancy and preparation by grandmothers the world over.

Waiting

There is certain business that's God's,
And His alone, I think,
And trying to outguess such grandeur
Seems to me at folly's brink.
And so I never mention signs
Or act as if I know;
In fact, in my expectant gladness
Both the tiny sexes grow.
Then when one comes I merely pause
To insure the other's keep,
Cradled warmly in my heart in
Softest gossamer of sleep.
For a little one is a precious thing
And I would not let one die,
Not even in a fragile dream
If I could help it with a sigh.

Knitting Now

Not in moccasins that glide in hogans,
Not in silken slippers of ballet,
You will come in sturdy, hump-toed brogans
Made in the old fashioned hard-sole way.
So your mother says, and wee soft bootees
Blue and pink I am knitting now with care;
She declares the little shoes you come in
Will no doubt be much too scuffed to wear.

Grandparents' welcome is a heartwarming part of those first few days at home with the new baby when the grandmother fills a special need and thinks her own yearning thoughts.

Remembering a Manger Scene

Would I have hastened with shepherds that holy night
To spread abroad the news to hearts afraid?
Or with the Magi, by divine insight
To my own country? No, I would have stayed
With Mary's little Child, I think, so I
Could help her marvel at His tiny feet,
Gently lift and tend Him at His cry,
And joy with her how fair He was, how sweet.

Grandfathers have their special brand of welcome, too. They may not be so much for frilly preparations, but after the actual product arrives, they are a bulwark of strength. Theirs are such commonsense actions as starting a savings account down at the bank in the new name. Or speaking up when it is needed, which may be even more sensible.

Long-Range Planning

They stand around him, the little new boy,
His family's pride and kinfolks' joy.
"Looks just like the Joneses," someone avers.
"Oh, I wouldn't say that!" another demurs.
"Look at the size of those hands and feet—
He's going to be a pro athlete."
"His lungs are strong; maybe he'll preach,
Or be a Senatah with old Southern speech."
"He'll wow the girls; just take a peek
At those big eyes and that physique!"
But while we are sending him off to frolic,
And mapping the life of the wee one with colic,
His granddad chucks him and winks an eye.
"You choose it, Skeeter, and we'll all stand by."

A little farther along, grandparents are for making grandchildren feel more wanted and secure in a world that at times can be cruel. This they do by various means. Sometimes, when they live close enough, they baby-sit.

One View

Everybody says how perfectly fitting
Grandparents are for the job of baby-sitting:
1. Always there
2. Really care
3. Don't want pay
4. Night or day
5. Children adore them
6. Don't have to implore them

Or grant them scandalous rights for fear they're quitting,
And they prefer it, don't they, just to *sitting*?

Confession of a Baby-Sitter

Baby-sitting is a new-coined word
jingling with modern sound, but behold
the prophet's patient keeping of Hannah's child
and Naomi's old age nourished by the son
of Ruth. And see young Miriam's sisterly eye
upon a bulrush cradle; and even Jesus
tenderly tending the little ones who were brought
to Him.
And in the horse-and-buggy days,
the straw-hat, ice-cream-suited days, there were
the baby-sitters who lived in—sometimes
a maiden aunt, a cousin, or granny who claimed
the children, and loved and spanked them as her own,
instilling morals by stern code.
At times
it was a bachelor uncle, a black sheep who
related eye-bugging tales of adventure as though
explaining why he had no children himself
to tell them to; or a bearded grandpa who
knew everything about the world, and could whittle
things of wondrous worth.
I think today
as always grandparents baby-sit because
they are expected to, and love tugs hard.
But honesty calls for truth. Most of them feel
nostalgia, "all of this and heaven, too!"

Sometimes grandparents read aloud from dog-eared books until their throats grow sore. Best loved, though, are the true stories they tell that star the little one listening with rapt attention and never tiring of hearing the story again and again.

The Accident

Undoubtedly again she will say,
"Nana, tell me about it all.
How the poor nurse let me fall."
And holding her closer to me still
As if to shield her from all ill,
I'll tell again of that first day.
"How big was I?"
"Oh, about that long."
"And was I in a in-cabater?"
"Yes, just born—and a little later—"
"What were they doing out in the hall
When the nurse let the in-cabater fall?"
"Going to weigh you."
"Did you hear a bong?"
"Oh, yes, but seeing it was worse.
We all saw it falling but couldn't do
A thing to stop it or rescue you.
Stunned and speechless and full of fear
We thought, 'This can't be happening here!' "
"But you felt sorry for the poor little nurse."

And I will nod. "It was heartrending
The way she stood there horrified
Then grabbed you up and bolted inside
The nursery where they ran a check—"
"But I wasn't hurt even one little speck!"
She will hasten to the happy ending.
And then like a hundred times before
We'll rock together a moment more
Before she asks, "Was an angel there
Guarding me, Nana, and is that why
I didn't get hurt?" She will hold my eye,
Knowing the answer, but wanting more.
And searching deep in the faith of my heart,
I will try again. "Yes, I think so.
To me it looked exactly as though
When you were falling, some gentle arm
Raised you and held you up from harm."
And so we will share our favorite part.

Next best loved are the stories about things that happened to grandparents and parents "when they were little." Although the identity of the characters in such dramas are not always immediately revealed, the enthralled young listeners seem almost intuitively to know. "That was you, Grandma." "Tell us about Granddad again."

Legacy

My grandma's snowy bed was smoothed to a mound,
And the truth was told, no matter what it cost
In her farmhouse, as clean as the tooth of a hound.
The shade of her reading lamp was as white as frost.
Without earth's wealth she left us something fine,
The gem of self-respect and cleanliness zest,
The silver lode of truth to maintain and mine,
And gold of love-for-learning to wisely invest.

Boy in Sunday Shoes

A boy in Sunday shoes let in the cows,
And as they grazed beneath a spire slim birch,
He imagined where sun sifted leafy boughs,
Like stained-glass windows, was a vaulted church,
A pea green mantis prayed within his reach,
A joyous bird choir sang "love never fails,"
And as a chipmunk took the stump to preach,
The grazing cows switched "amen" with their tails.

Spring Tonic

The new-plowed row was a shiny rope
Swung in the sun for a boy's proud hope
Of walking its length without a fall
As he waved his arms, and watching it all,
A tree-squatter crow let the whole world know
About some shoes at the end of the row.
Hush up, old crow, and you'd better heed;
I'll tell on you when you steal seed!

Sometimes grandparents sing. The genius of grandparent-singing is that they can plagiarize to their hearts' content, and no one will object. For instance, the words of the following lullaby can be altered to fit any situation. The tune can be improvised on the spot, lifted bodily from another song, or be a medley of gospel songs, as the spirit moves. Grandparents know this. And so they sing, to sleepy little forms cuddled against them in complete trust and contentment.

Rocking Song

Little sweet one, precious dear,
precious dear, oh, precious dear,
Little sweet one, precious dear,
Good Lord keep from harm and fear.

Mommy and Daddy love you true,
love you true, oh, love you true,
Mommy and Daddy love you true,
and all the kinfolks love you, too.

You're our little pumpkin pie,
pumpkin pie, oh, pumpkin pie,
You're our little pumpkin pie,
Nana loves you, me, oh, my!

Pawpaw thinks you're mighty fine,
mighty fine, oh, mighty fine,
Pawpaw thinks you're mighty fine,
you're his real live valentine.

Little one now needs to sleep,
needs to sleep, oh, needs to sleep,
Little one now needs to sleep,
Gentle Jesus, watch and keep.

For you love her, too, we know,
too we know, oh, too, we know,
For you love her, too, we know,
this sweet baby we love so.

When grandparents sing, it may not always be a melodious rendition. (It seldom is.) But to the grandchildren listening, the sound, however lacking, has its own special message.

Dialogue With God

I've always liked to sing, Father. You know that.

Aloud?

Yes, dear Lord. Oh, I've never been a Kate Smith or a Jenny Lind, but when I was younger, I didn't sound so bad.

But the song that I gave you is the song of the written word. Just because you are a grandmother now doesn't change that.

I want to thank you, anyway, Dear Father.

For what, dear child?

For giving me grandchildren to sing to. It has meant the revival of my singing.

But you still get to heist a tune at church, though—harumph! I admit I've had to send an angel several times of late to straighten out some of your notes before I let them sound. Are you sure—?

Very sure, dear Father. Oh, I know my voice cracks sometimes now and isn't pretty anymore, but my grandchildren like it. And, Father?

Yes, child.

I think it's because my grandchildren hear all the love that's in my singing. And that makes the difference.

Ah, yes, my child!

And of course, grandparents are for taking and showing pictures of their grandchildren, which they do with proud abandon and no embarrassment—and proper detailed explanations. They display them on walls, tables, pianos, and mantels at home. They carry them in purses and billfolds for "instant" showing when away from home.

There are those of the baby, like the one in the nude.

Please Don't Drink the Bath Water

Little bathing beauty bare,
Splashing water everywhere,
Accompanied by a retinue
Of baubles made to bathe with you,
Subject them to aquatic slaughter,
But please don't drink your own bath water!

Dunk the butcher and the baker
And the hapless candlestick maker;
Hold your rubber duck tail up
And douse him from your plastic cup;
Taste the soap, though you hadn't oughter,
But please don't drink your own bath water!

And sometimes there are two.

Twins

Two babes at once! Oh, my, how nice
To have such sweetness given twice.
Four little feet instead of two,
Four little hands to guide to do;
Two little hearts to guard and keep
And teach a lay-me-down-to-sleep;
Four starry eyes to look into
When once-upon-a-times are through;

A pair of hurts to kiss and tell
To never mind, it will soon be well;
And two tight hugs to let one see
How much "I love you" means to be.
To watch one tiny life unfold
Is worth a miser's pot of gold,
But seeing two go hand in hand
I think must be the grandest grand.

And there are those at the age when they have begun to look all legs.

Jeanie

You are
like a blossom
that unfolds its petals,
and we watching, think, oh, surely
this of all the different
stages
is the loveliest of a young girl's
ages.
You were
yesterday an
exquisite bud, unopened,
and tomorrow—suddenly!—you will
stand before us a full blown
flower.
We shall weep but softly in that
hour.
Now you
are a golden
Brown, longlegged sprite who
dances
in our hearts.

And there are group pictures, like the gangling cast of the school play (including, of course, the outstanding member of the entire posed group).

School Christmas Play

Mary is weeping, for one of the Magi,
His towel turban devilishly awry,
Has torn her shawl. The angels' wings
Keep falling off; the girl who sings
The cradle song has a sniffly cold,
And Joseph's beard looks crooked and old.
The shepherds with their squirms and probes
Are just small boys in dads' bathrobes,
While the moving star in a last minute try
Has jumped its track and leapt from the sky.
Then with a final scramble and hunt,
It is curtain time, and out in front,
Parents and grandparents sit with fear
The Christmas play will "flop" this year.
Then lights, and reverently serene
And beautiful, the manger scene
Looks blessedly real, till even they
Who were backstage in the bedlam and fray
Are caught in the spell, and all realize
A miracle is happening before their eyes—
A once-a-year miracle enabling men
To worship with shepherds and Magi again.

And when everyone else has finished, there is the picture Granddad always gets around to pulling out of his wallet.

Star of the Team

Now when on earth did he ever grow
That length behind his punting toe?
Why, only yesterday he chewed
On bootees in which he was shoe-ed,
Then raced in sneakers like a whizz!
These man-sized shoes just can't be his.
And yet they are, we know, aware
He's just our grandson, but out there
He's quite a hero, it would seem,
The star, they say, of all the team!

Grandparents are for listening for grandchildren (a habit practiced so long they have grown to be experts in it).

Through the Years

At first we only napped at night, our ears attuned to hear
The slightest movement of the wee sprawled bodies sleeping near.
"When they are older we'll stop listening for them so," we said,
But still we listened as each baby outgrew the baby bed
And moved with grown-up airs into a bedroom of his own.
Pretending not to listen then, we said, "when they are grown,"
Each thinking that the day was far, but in no time at all
We saw one off to woo his maid, another to a ball
With her prince charming; and together long night hours through,
Each felt a comfort knowing that the other listened, too.
"When they are married," we said then, attempting to be gay,
"I guess we'll quit this listening," but again it is past that day,
And now we listen for the sound of an approaching car
That brings small ones to hug our necks and raid the cookie jar.

When grandchildren are still young, their grandparents are great fountains of sympathy in which they can bathe away the little hurts and woes of their small lives. As they grow up, those same grandparents often become streams into which they can pour the problems too shocking to share with anyone else, even parents. With teenage discernment they know somehow that grandparents will listen with the same loving sympathy and understanding they gave them as children.

Listening

Listening is not merely
Catching words in sound
Then passing them on quickly
For careless tossing around.

It is a sense of treasuring
Another's fault or dream
Like coins that are dropped in
Deep waters of a stream.

It is a way of knowing
Which coins to draw out
And which to leave in silence
With minnow swarm and trout.

Grandparents especially
Are shaded streams of heart,
And few there are who excel them
In the lovely listening art.

Grandparents are also for spoiling grandchildren. At least, the old saw says, "Spoil them; then give them back to their parents." It's been around so long that many believe it. Most grandparents, however, are aware of another reason, which is the real one behind their readiness to "give them back."

Question Answered

At first grandparents may question
With apprehension wrung
Why God entrusted *their* grandchild
To two so green and young.

Then down remembrance's roadway
Reliving their young years
They know now how they must have seemed
To those with similar fears.

And called again to battle
With limbs grown heavy as stones
They fold their tents and slip away
To rest their weary bones.

Grandparents have their own concept of spoiling, and you can rest assured it is not your usual run of the mill notion.

Sweet Clutter

When toys and little clothes are strewn galore,
And on a table, bottle lies with didy,
When pots and pans are spread on kitchen floor,
Some people want to call a house untidy,
But not grandmothers. Retrieving small scuffed shoes
And sweeping up stray cracker crumbs, they mutter,
"Untidy, fiddlesticks!" Then like good news,
"Everybody knows it's just sweet clutter!"

Never a Dull Moment

March is the boisterous, mischievous grandson
Of Grandma Winter, and on her last call
She brings him along, a rip-roaring cowboy
Who whoops and hollers through room and hall.
He is two-gun Deadeye, but we are indulgent,
Though he leaves gunpowder on table and sill;
For what salts a day and adds to it ginger
Like a breeze, or a boy, that cannot be still?

In fact, according to grandparents, a certain kind of spoiling is necessary and apropos of the purpose for grandparents.

Spoiling

Spoiling is not the same as loving a child,
Though grandparents are sometimes the ogres grim
Who make a model of discipline wantonly wild
With just some cookies and two hours spent with them!

Grandchildren need the special kind of love
In "a bushel and a peck, and—" the kind
Grandparents have left over and above—
The easy rocking-chair type so hard to find.

There are times that grandparents should beware—
The break-of-parental-rule-and-doting times—
But no amount of real love will impair.
It gives the bell of childhood sweetest chimes.

Surely, in the main, grandparents are for watching grandchildren grow. Everyone needs a "booster band," as it was once called—a cheering section that believes in and stands behind and cheers on, in victory or defeat. Athletic coaches know this. And grandparents know it, too. So they stand on the sidelines, not the first team anymore, but playing their important part as they watch with various supporting emotions:

Protectively–

Prayer Thought

What makes you look so vulnerable,
Small baby boy just come,
When all the world shouts, "It's a boy!"
And beats the herald drum?
Is it because of wars to fight
Almost before you grow?
Is it the strength your own man-world
Demands that you must show?
Is it because your little body
Clinging to me here
Is filled with courage, to be sure,
But also shares my fear?
O God, our help, may wars be stilled
When he is strong and tall,
And may he give his heart to Thee,
His life, his dreams, his all.

Crawler

I judge the one who called it crawling or creeping
  would have described a steamer as treading
  and a jet as hovering.
Scampering is more like it
  or scooting
  or hastening or hieing.
She waves bye-bye and then is off
  to find another wonder
  to get into.
But even "months" must seek their independence
  must strive to find and know
  on their own.
And so we loosen the cord a little
  and move a few more things.
We are always moving to higher ground
  these days, it seems.
No, it isn't a flood—
  just a crawler
  touching the world.

Adoringly–

One Year Old

One year old is a wonderful age
For a little girl to be,
For a world of wonderful things await
For a little girl to see
And point a tiny finger toward
And reach to pull or feel,
Or sometimes take a taste to find
If they will make a meal.
And there are places to travel to
By crawling leaps and bounds
Or trying out two wobbly legs
With sudden sitting downs,
And people watched in solemnness
Until gone out of sight,
Then given wave of chubby arm
And "Hi!" of pure delight.
One year old is a wonderful age,
And a little girl must know
Somehow how very much she is loved.
Dear God, O help her grow!

Head Patting Size

A small boy's head is at the place
Where grownup folks can reach and pat,
And everytime they come near him
They reach right out and do just that.
But though he squirms, he does not mind
So much, it seems, just shakes it loose
Not even looking up to find
Who did the patting. Now what is there
About a sturdy little boy
That merely touching his tousled head
Gives grownups such a grinning joy?

Wonderingly—

Love Affair

What alchemy at work upon your genes
Preceding birth gave you the rare insight
To recognize protective, gentle love
In this big man who swings you to such height?
You gaze down on us, smugness in small face
As if to say, "Look what my daddy's doing!"
But if some other dares swing you as high,
Your tears instead of squealing leaves him ruing.
The love affair between this giant man
And tiny you, you seem to take in stride,
And may it always be between you two—
A love of gentleness and shining pride.

Before the Robins

The world outside was a misty day
With gusty winds and clouds at bay.
He stopped his play there long enough
To breeze inside for small boy stuff,
Then bang out, leaving in my care
His sweater I had made him wear.
And while I said, "Too cold for Spring,"
He touched her hand, high in his swing.

Delightedly—

Boy on an Errand

Spying such things
As gossamer wings
And gunning his plane to catch them in flight,
Or watching a mouth
Of iron turning south
To scoop up half of the earth in a bite,
A boy, unaware,
Is never there,
By the time you think he ought to be,
But surely you know
Why he tarries so—
There is God's whole wonderful world to see.

Saying Grace

I know a small girl who gives thanks to God
For every item of food upon the table
Except for spinach and okra, and to thank him for them
She simply is not hypocritically able.
She takes a look around at every dish
And names it as she says the mealtime prayer,
And thinks it not amiss to stop and ask,
"Mother, what's that in that bowl right there?"
But I like best the time she included all—
Dishes, silver, napkins—then opening one eye
And closing it said with greatest piousness,
"And for that bite Bud just took on the sly."

Yearningly—

Young Girl Called Twice

Curled in the luxury of a dream,
She sighs when called and fighting wishes,
Slowly emerges. I know it must seem
Foolish to her that in life's scheme
A dream must wait on washing dishes.

And yet the task awaits her here,
It is hers to do for a little while,
And as duty teaches her heart to steer,
The light of her dream, still burning clear,
Will sail with duty many a mile.

Left Behind

We used to show you the moon far, far away,
And lifting chubby arms up high, you would say,
"Way-way!" as moonlight bathed your baby face.
But now as you lift excited teenage eyes,
And speak of the moon in travel miles and size,
You frighten us—belonging so to space!

and Compassionately—

First Love

Grandson, why are your eyes so stilled
As if by starlight they are filled?
Are you awed by the wonder inside you there,
Half deep fear and half deep prayer?
When did your face so small-boy clean
Grow tender-mouthed? What does it mean?
Did you find a young girl fairer still
And race with her up a flowered hill?
And then did she suddenly vanish away,
The maiden who entered your dream today—
Blend with the gentle, pattering rain,
The new-green hill and your heart's sweet pain?
Grandson, you will find her again,
Fairest of fair among daughters of men.
She waits for you in the far-off springs,
And your heart will know by the song it sings.

Shared Anguish

Today I saw your teenage woe
And knew the hurt I could not stop
With kiss or bandaid laid on top
Of scratch or bump or small stubbed toe.

And suddenly I was made aware
Of the day your mother came to know
The truth you learned today—to grow
Is sometimes anguish one must bear.

I felt you thought I should have cures
By now, this second time around;
But when your anguishes abound
I still can only pain with yours.

Yet, in spite of all the foregoing, grandparents may sometimes feel that there isn't much reason they are left on earth in the first place. And in the second place, there isn't much they can do to fulfill even that destiny. Or is there?

It All Adds Up

There isn't much grandparents are for,
But they can make it all seem par
By saying, better scratched up car
Than some young hide somebody's skinning,
And start your parents into grinning.

There isn't much grandparents are for,
But they can place a steady bar
In front of folly's gate ajar,
And though you fume at fogey stuff,
The bar remains there, strong enough.

There isn't much grandparents are for,
But they can show you in life's war
How you can live with wound and scar
And never whimper or declare
That life's too hard or God unfair.

There isn't much grandparents are for,
But they can tell you of a Star
That shined one night for sins that mar,
And make it sound so real and right
Your heart will see it, clear and bright.

Finally, grandparents are for praying, which they do with ever increasing faith in the Providence that watches over the affairs of men.

Sublimest Calling

Of all the things that grandparents may be for,
I think to make appeal at Heaven's bar
Is their sublimest calling.

I know that praying has no year-marked gauge,
But surely faith mounts up along with age
When gold the leaves are falling.

And while the young their highest mountain climb
And lend their zeal to building empires, time
Gives age a reflective hour.

And like two old friends in their drawn-up chairs,
Age talks with God about life's joys and cares—
And His great grace and power.

Prayer for a Young Couple Who Now Are Parents

Thank you for being our Lord and Savior.

Thank you that they belong to you, too, Dear Father.

Thank you for giving both of us these, their children and our sweet grandchildren.

Keep them, O Lord, ever faithful and true to each other, and to you.

And grant them, O God, the wisdom and patience and know-how to bring these little ones to a saving knowledge of Jesus, and to rear them well. In His name we ask. Amen.

And now, as the Preacher of Ecclesiastes stated it, "Let us have the conclusion of the whole matter." He then proceeded to sum up his profound subject in these succinct words, "Fear God, and keep his commandments: for this is the whole duty of man." It is doubtful that my summary will be as excellent. For who can compress into one poem the oftentimes lovable, admirable, gracious, kind, mature, salty, gallant, and sometimes cantankerous human beings who are grandparents? Well, I shall try.

Who Are Grandparents and What Are They For?

They *are*. But what are grandparents for?
Not to be the guiding star,
But to add dimension to its gleam.

Not to try to make into
With zeal, as parents sometimes do,
But to listen to a tender dream.

Not to brag of the good old days,
But to be a pleasant stream of ways
Where youth can pan its own bright gold.

Not to preach of piety,
But to *be*, so even a child can see
The wonder of God's love unfold.